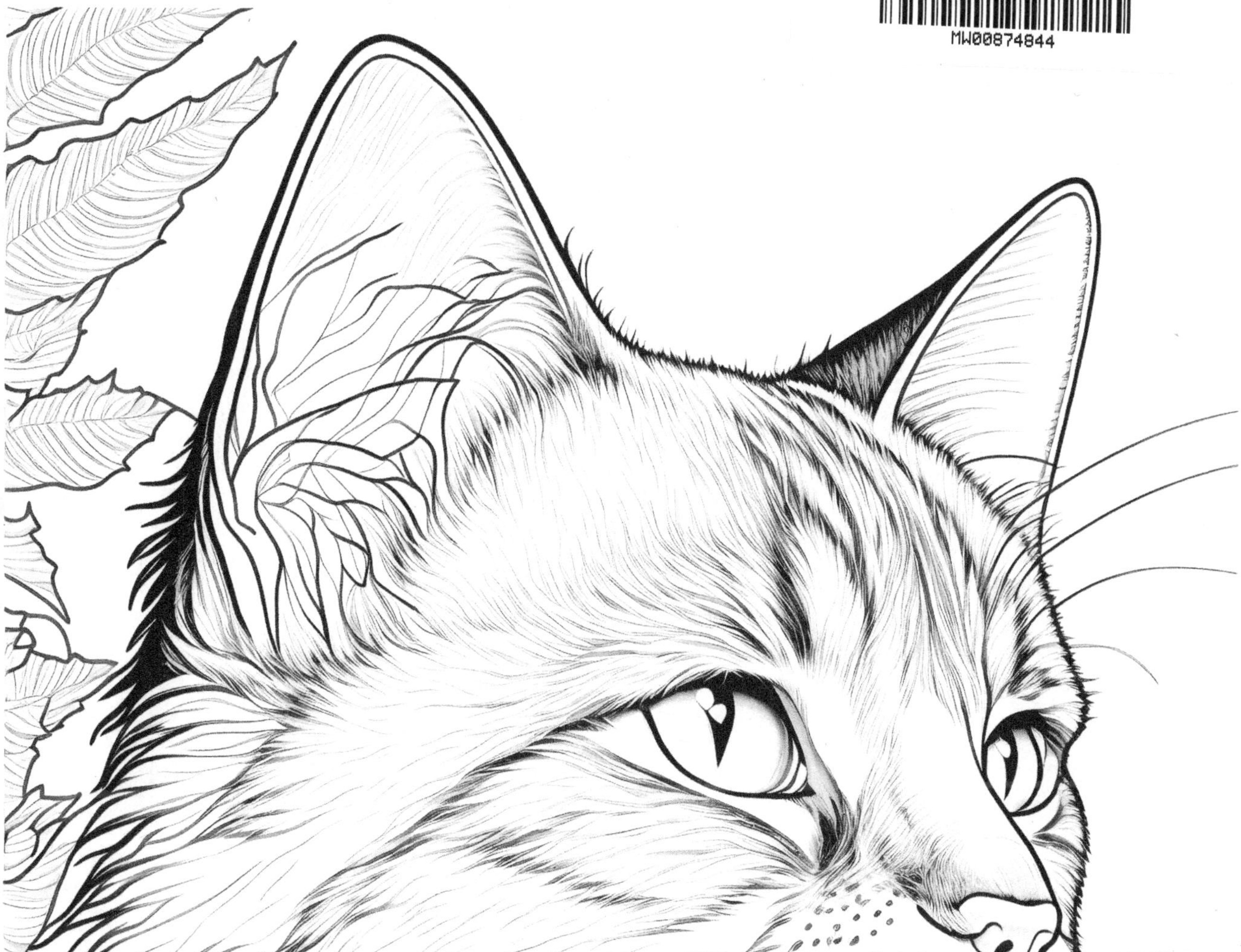

LARGE PRINT

CAT COLORING BOOK

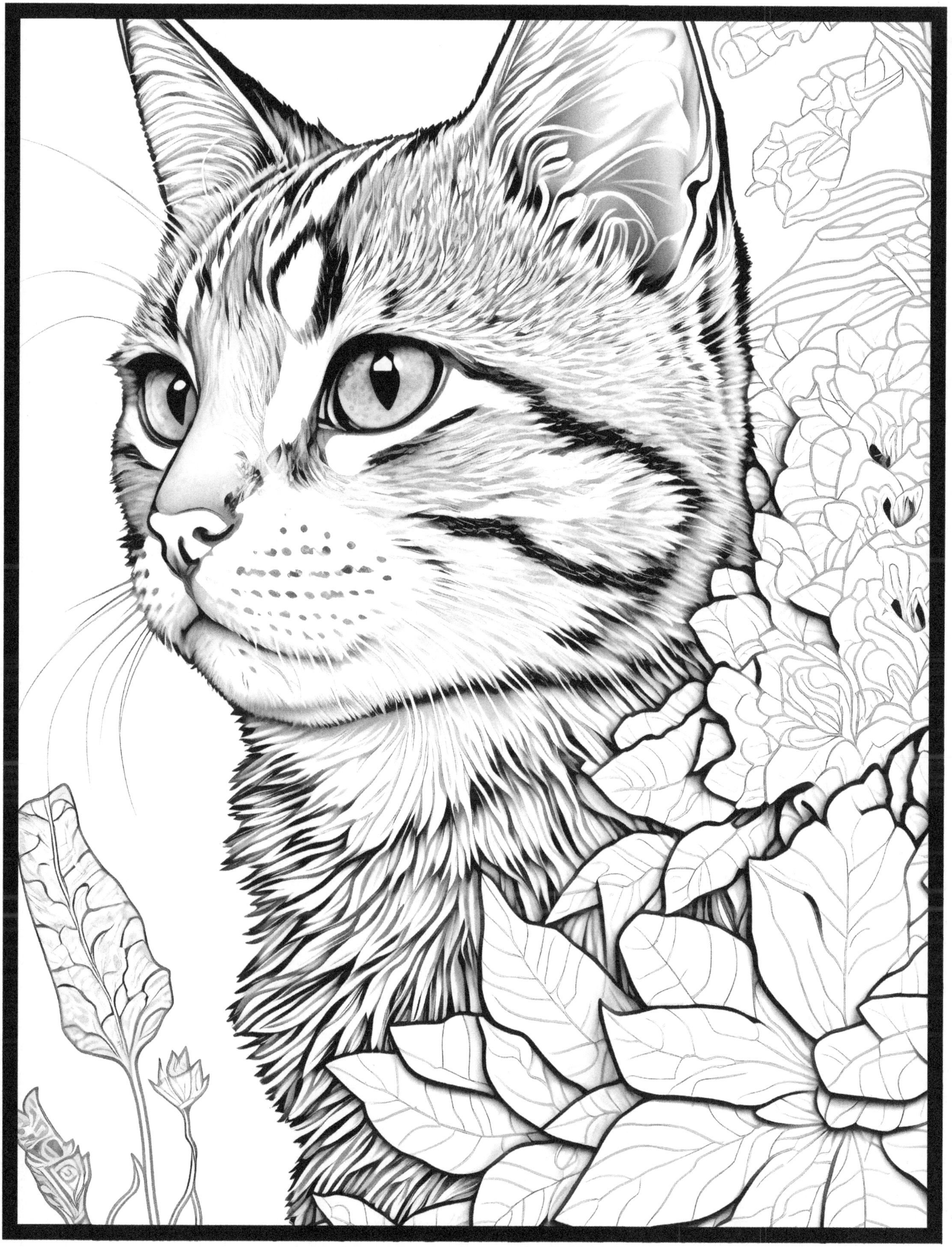

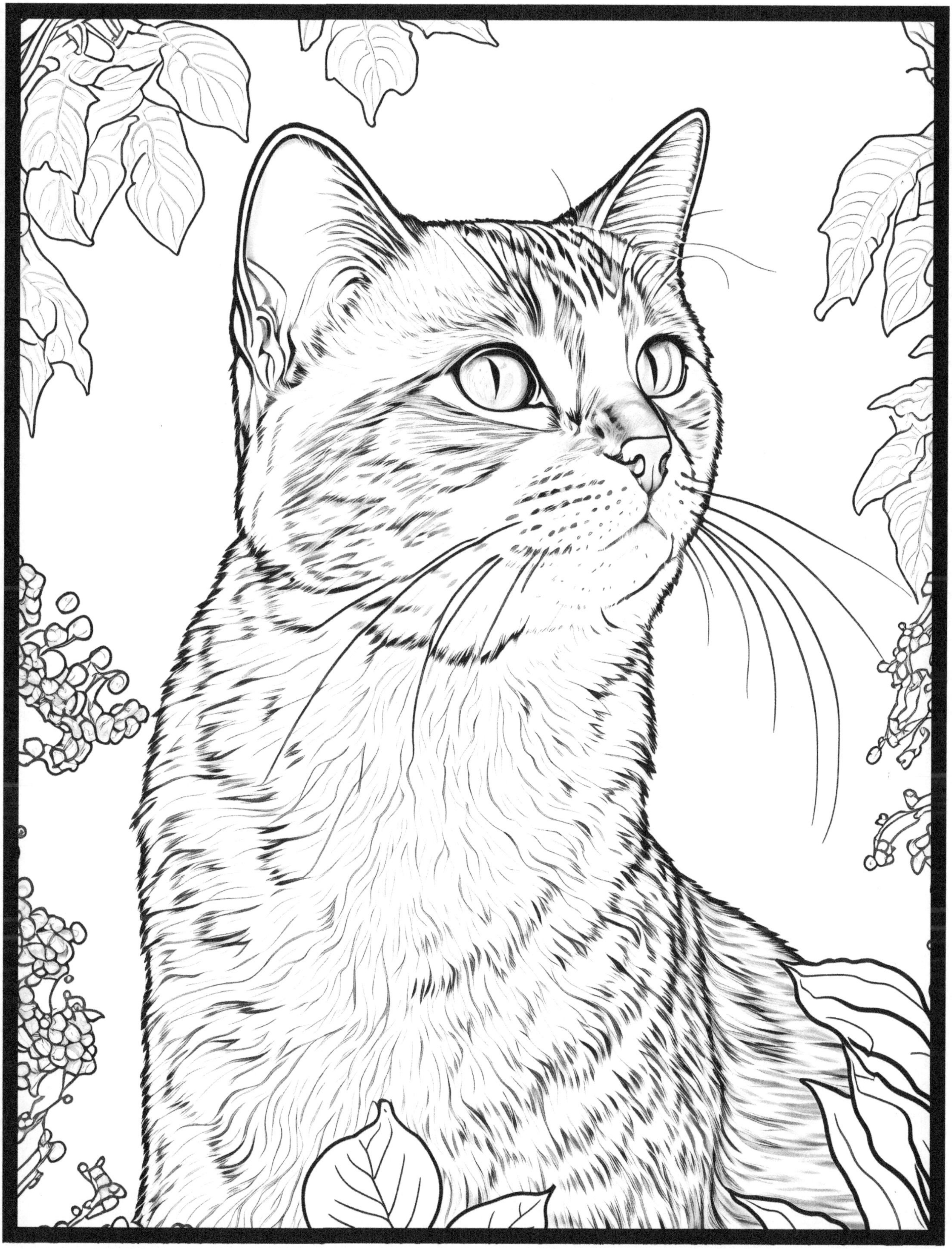

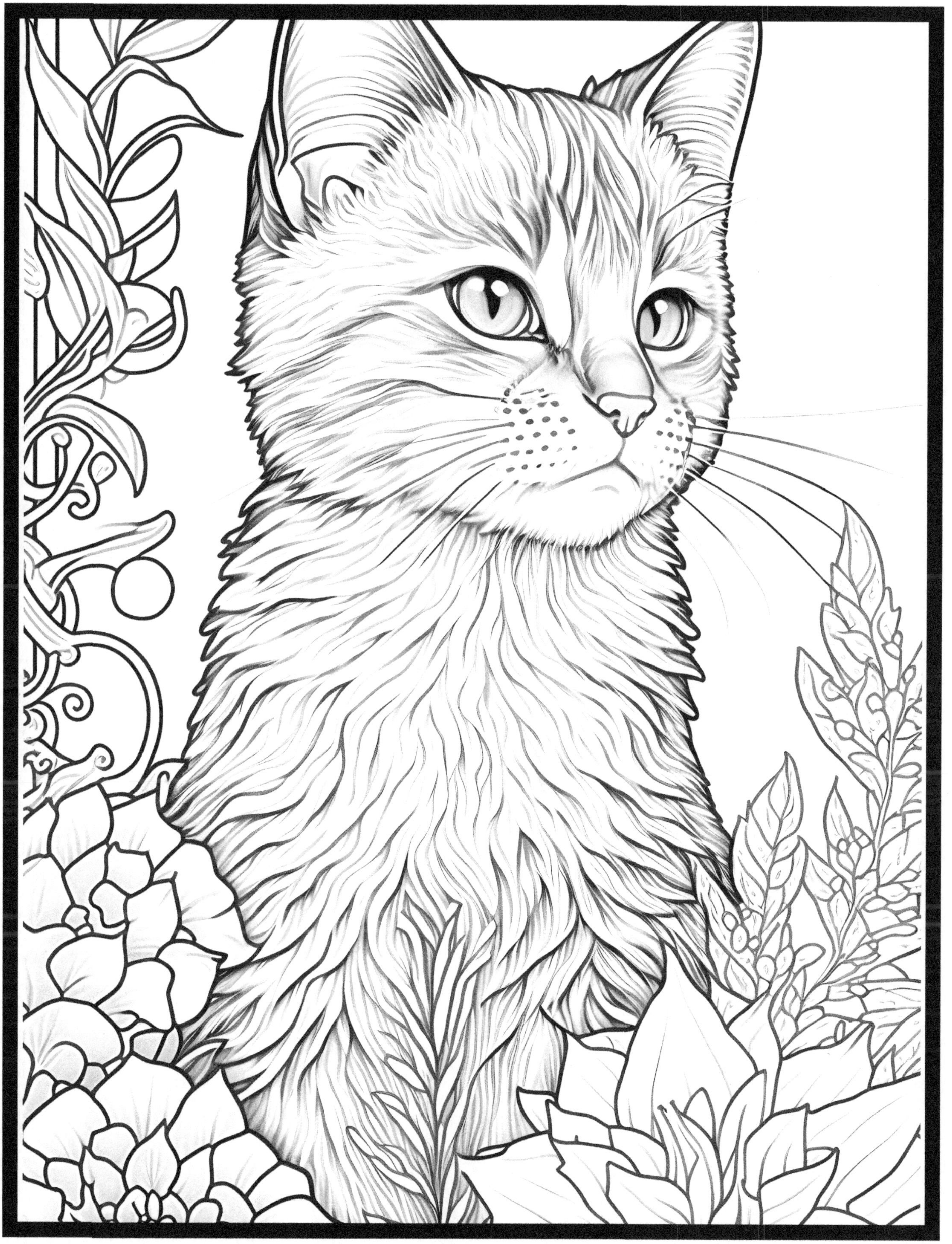

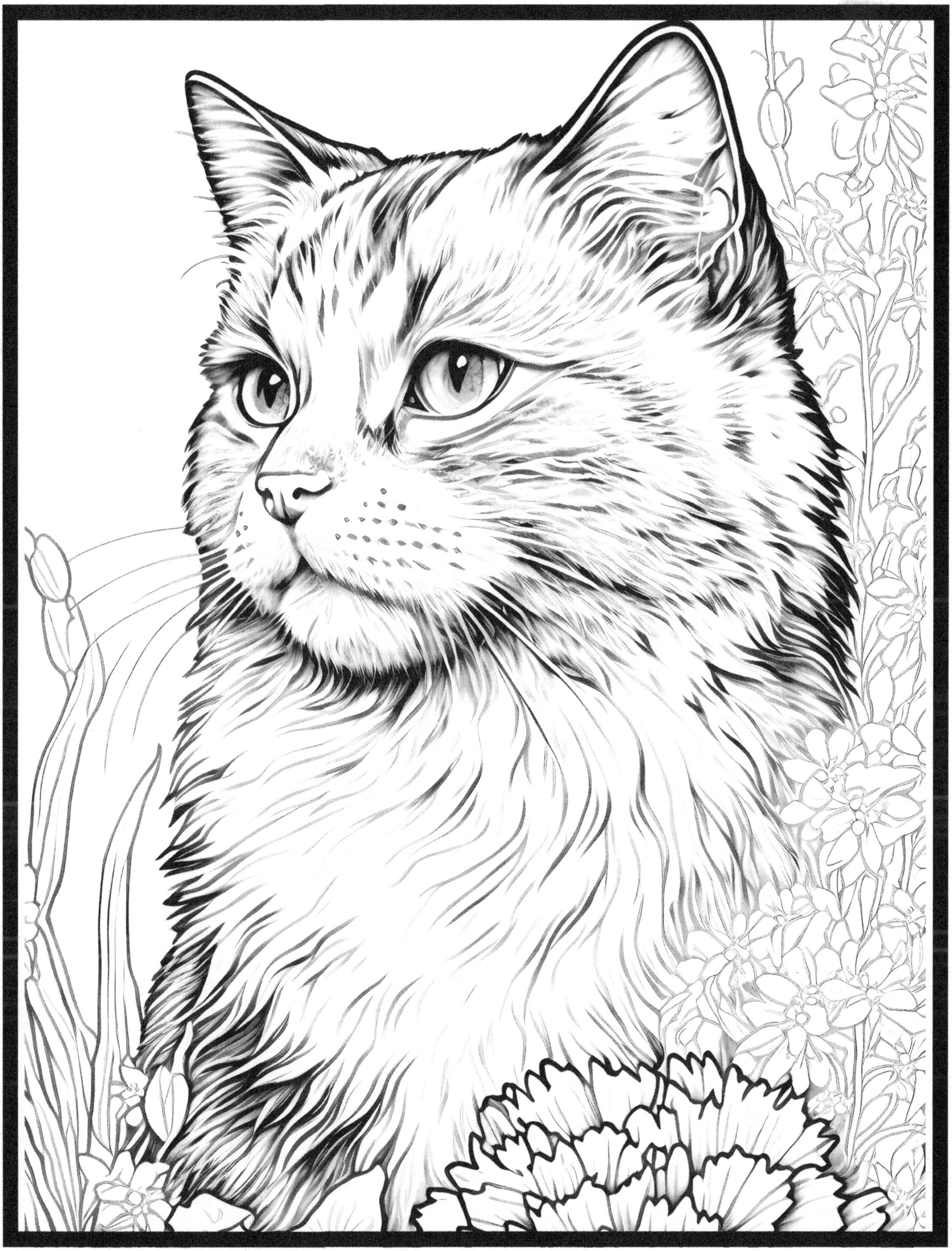

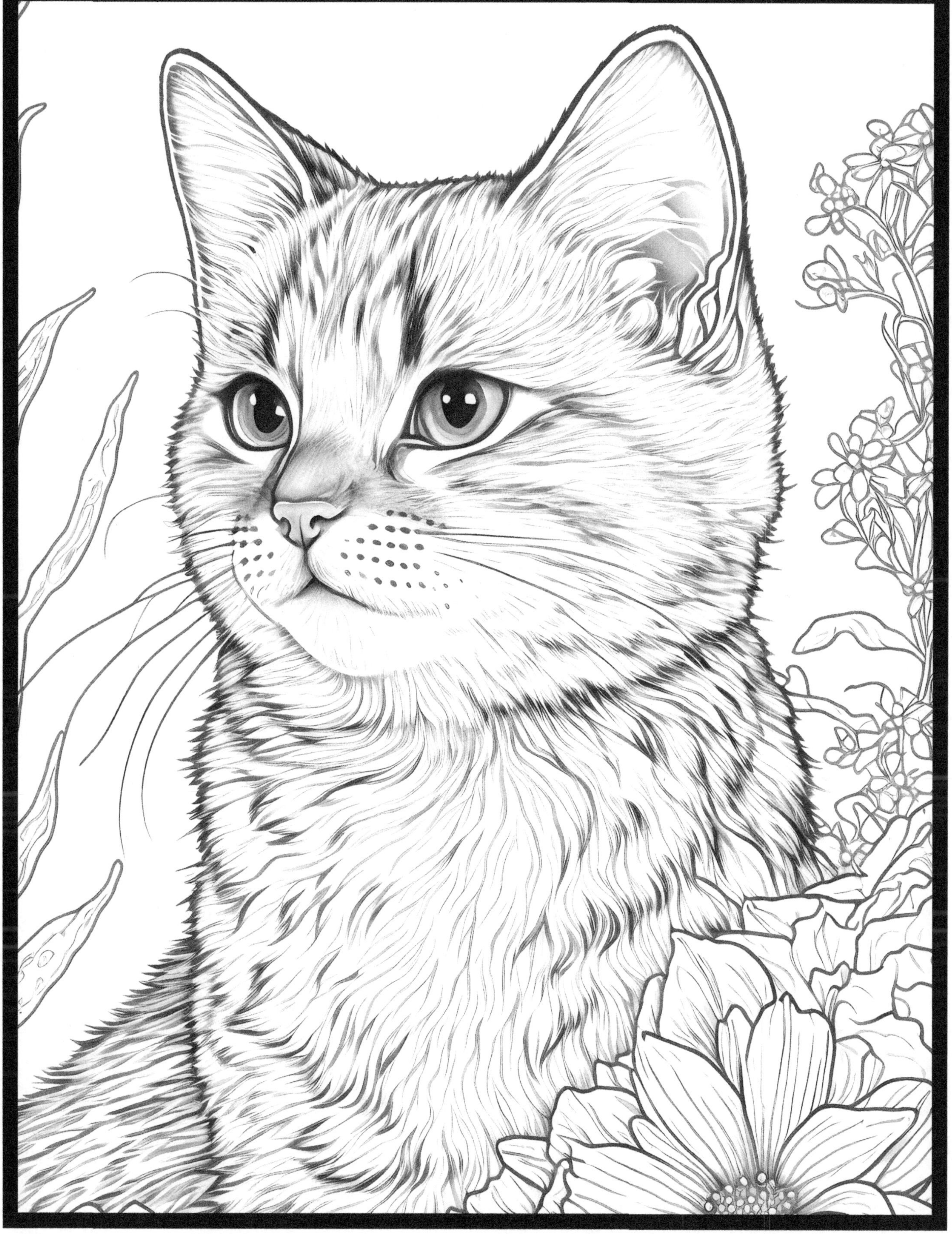

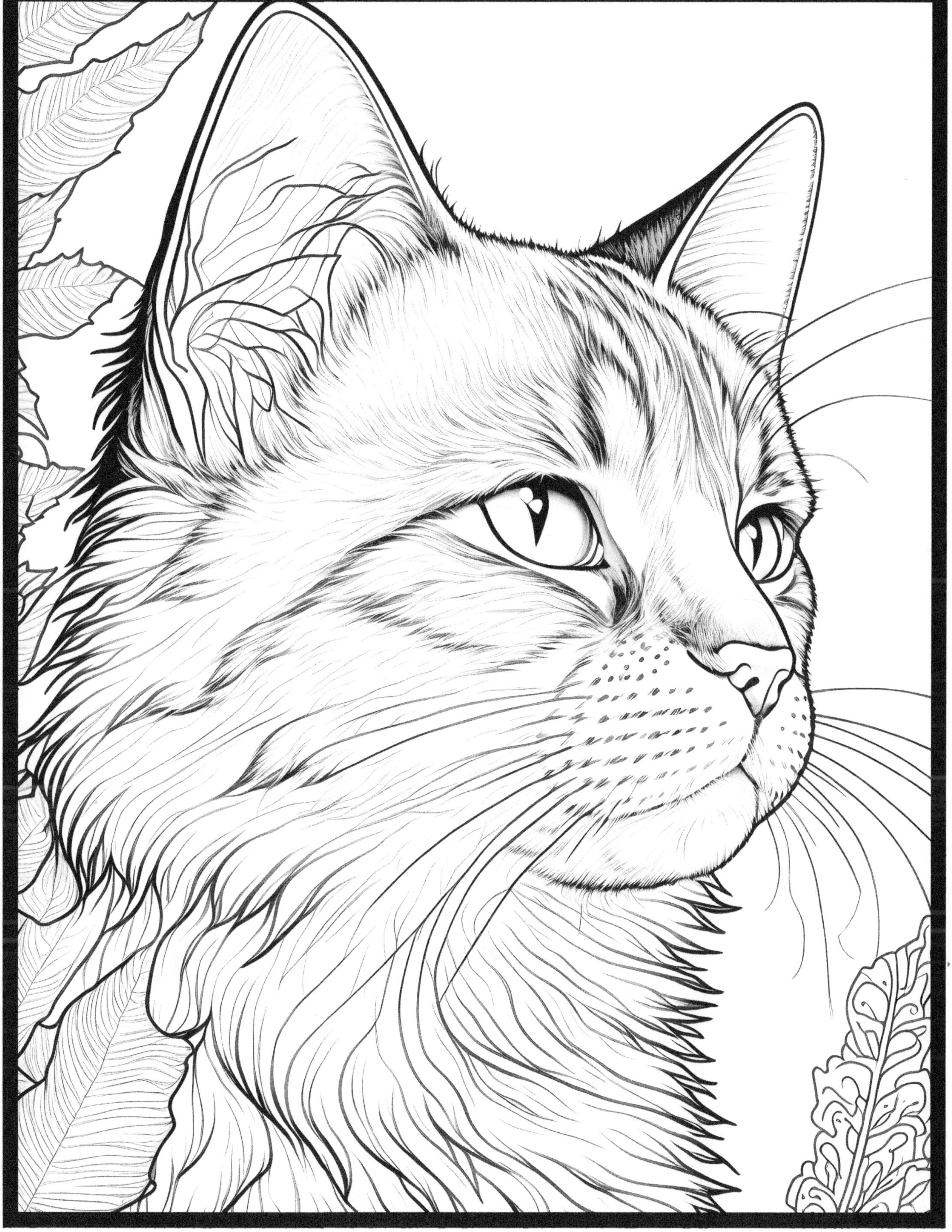

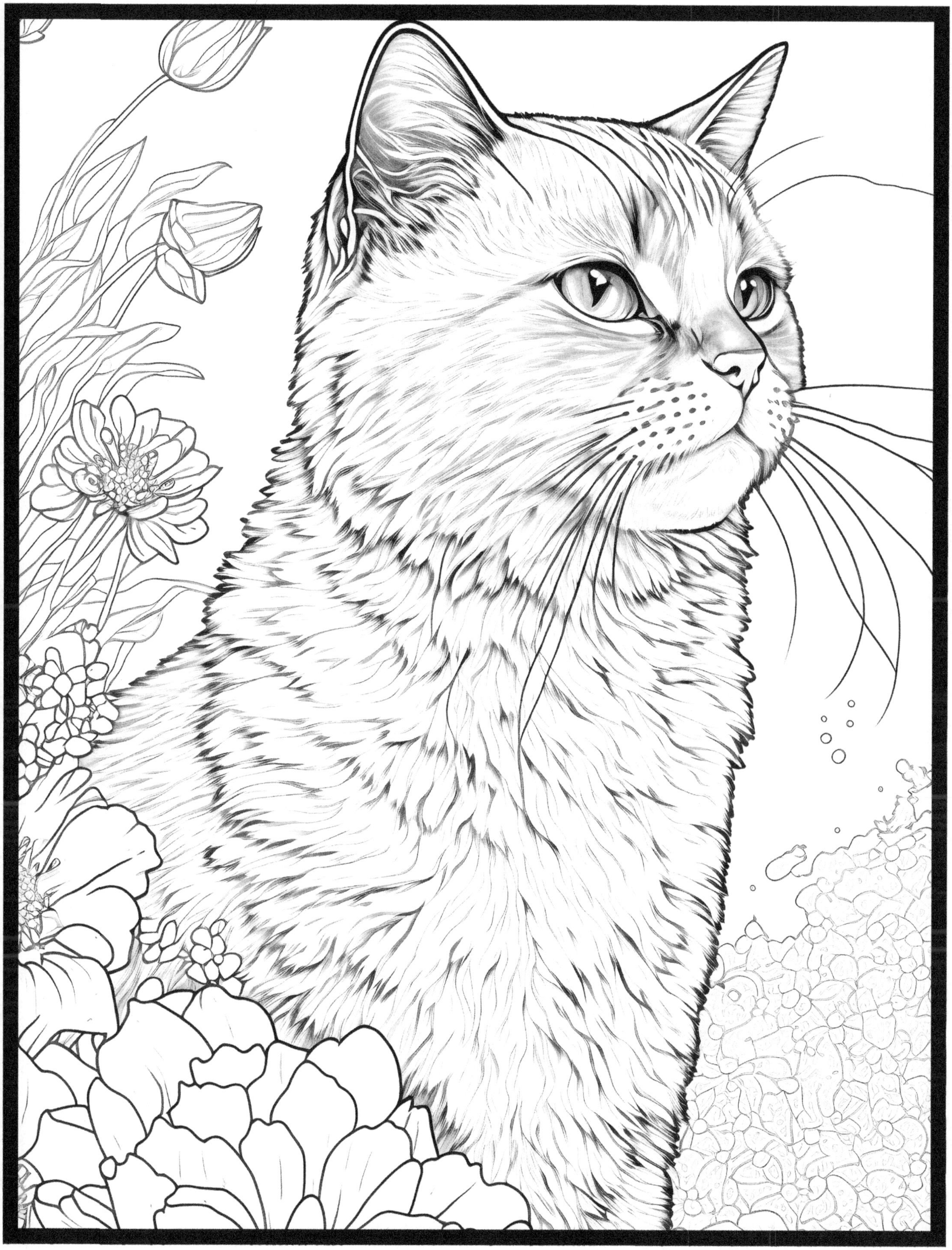

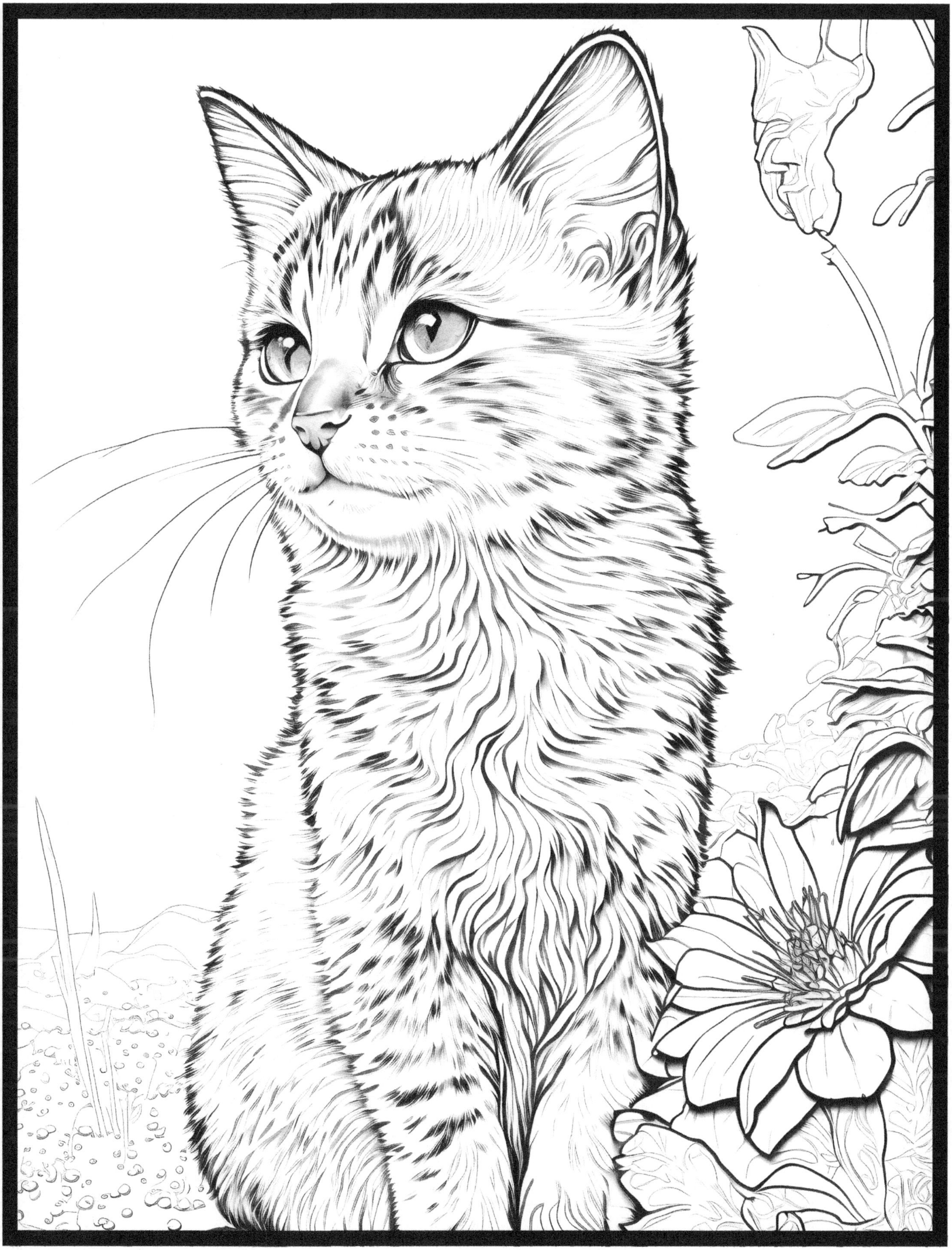

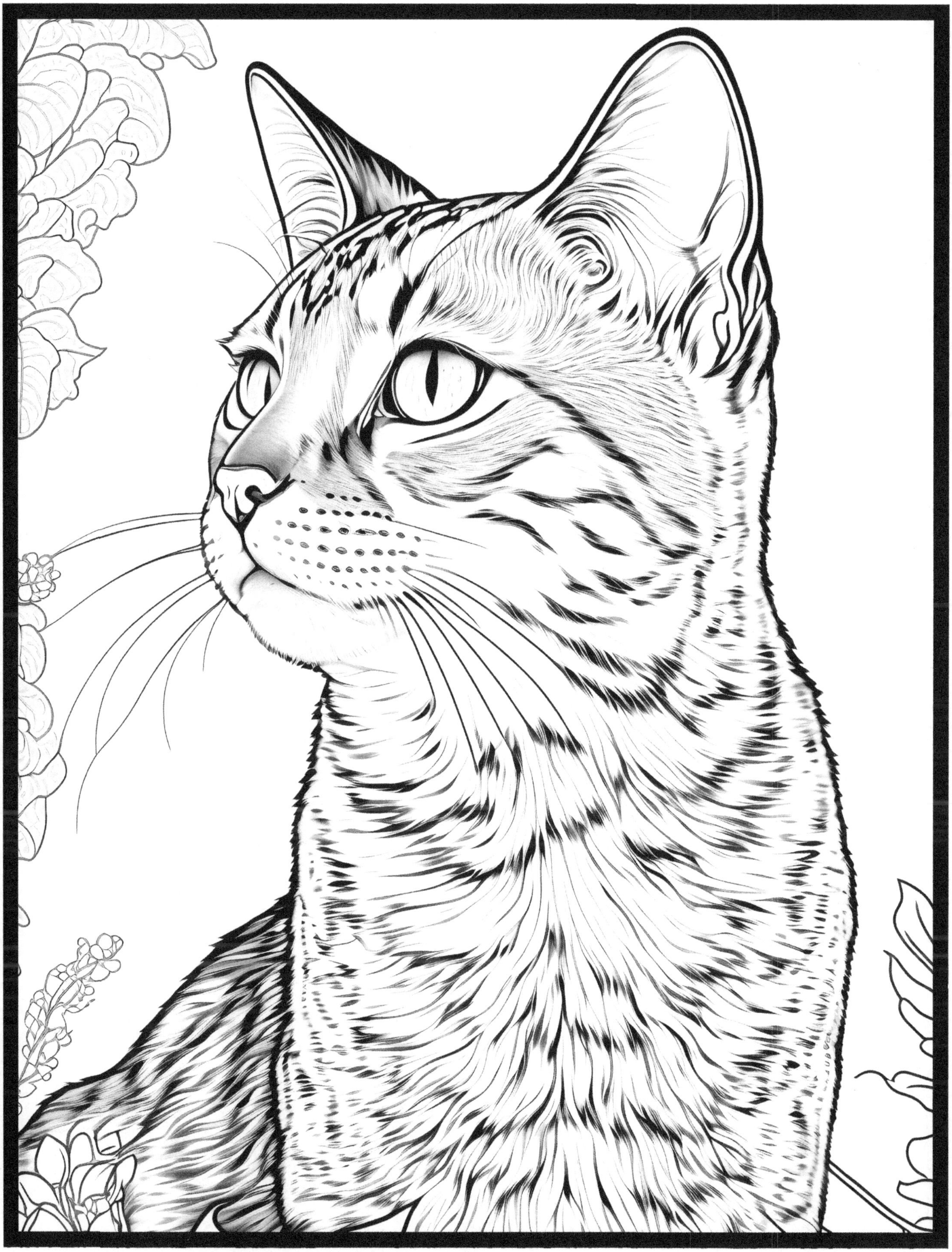

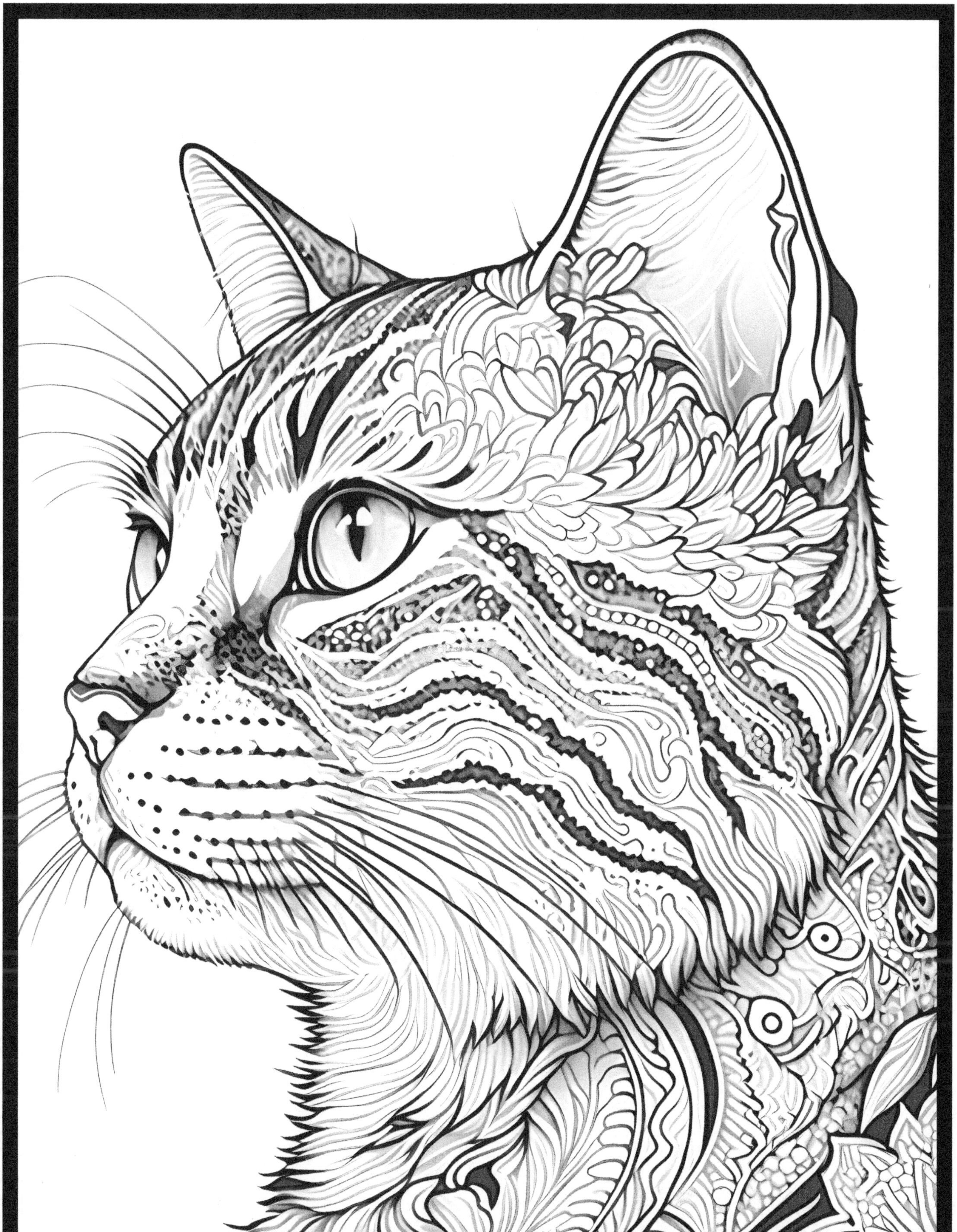

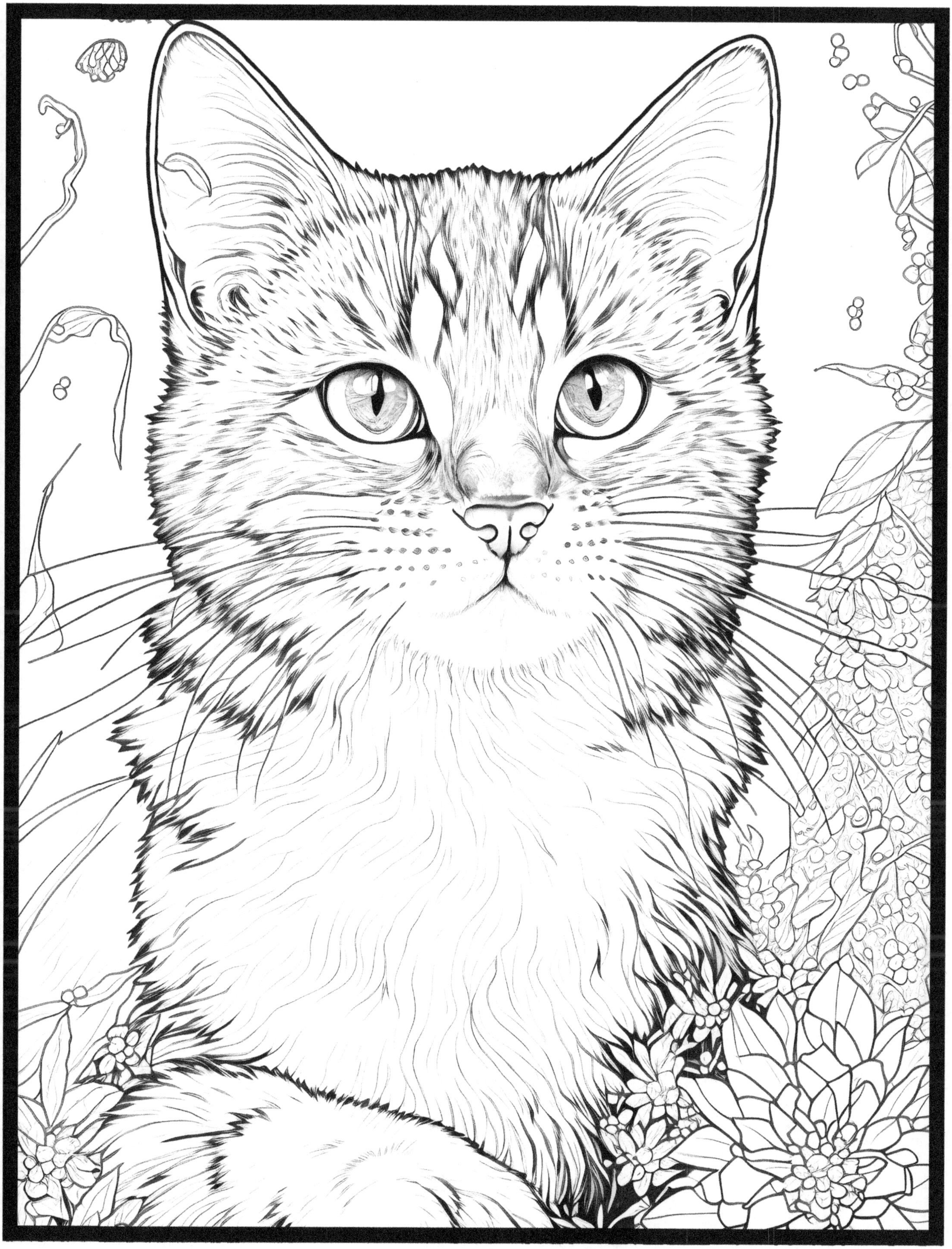

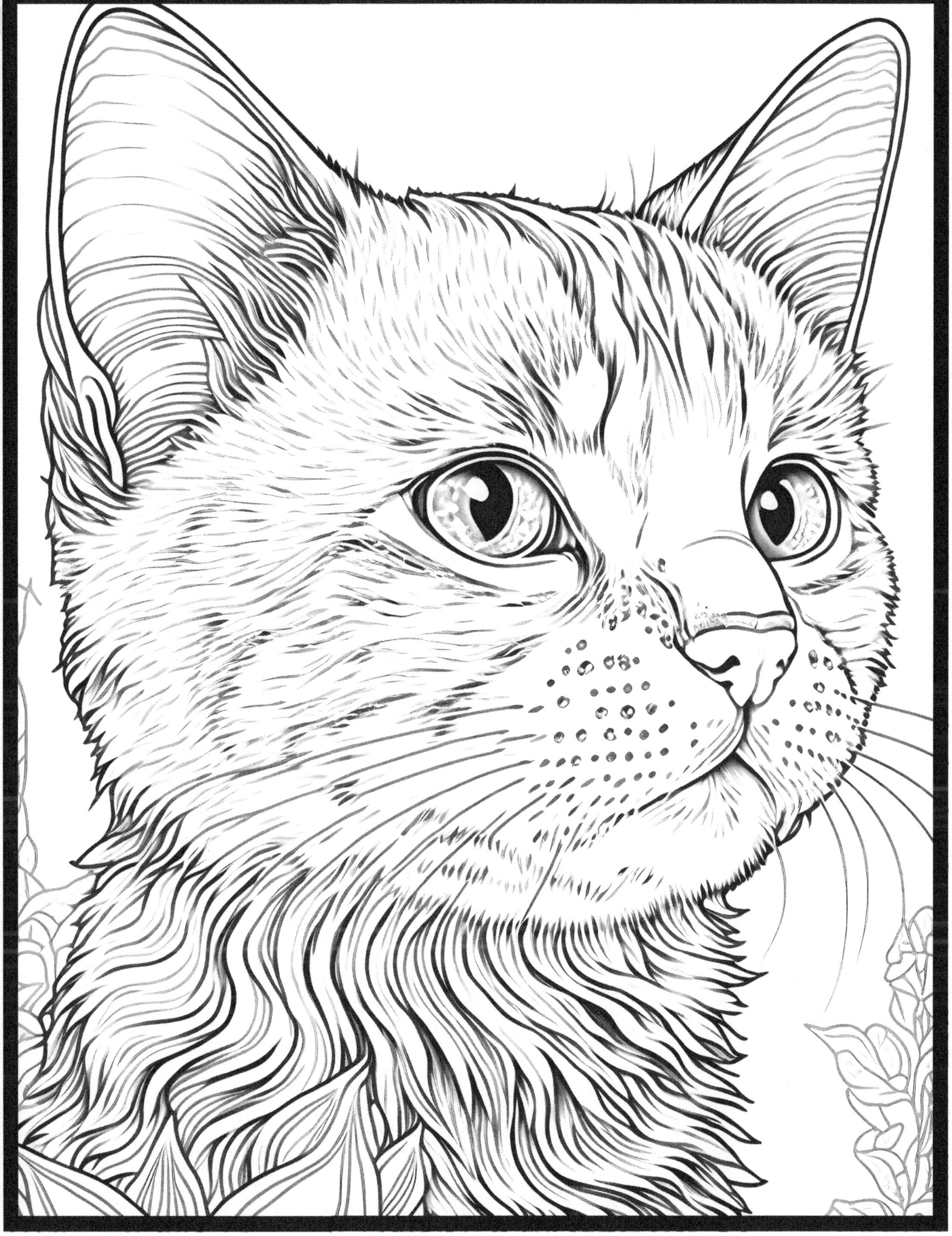

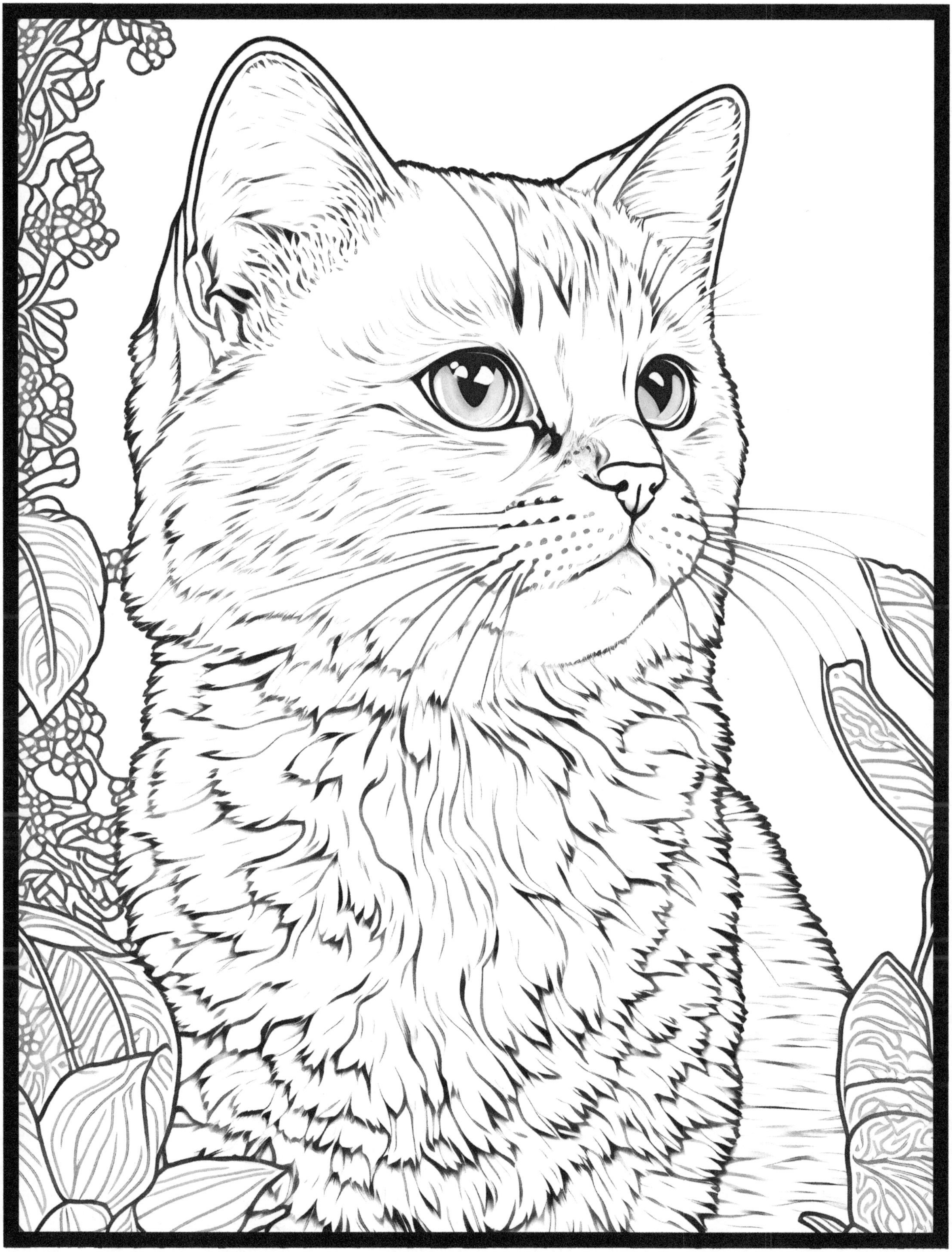

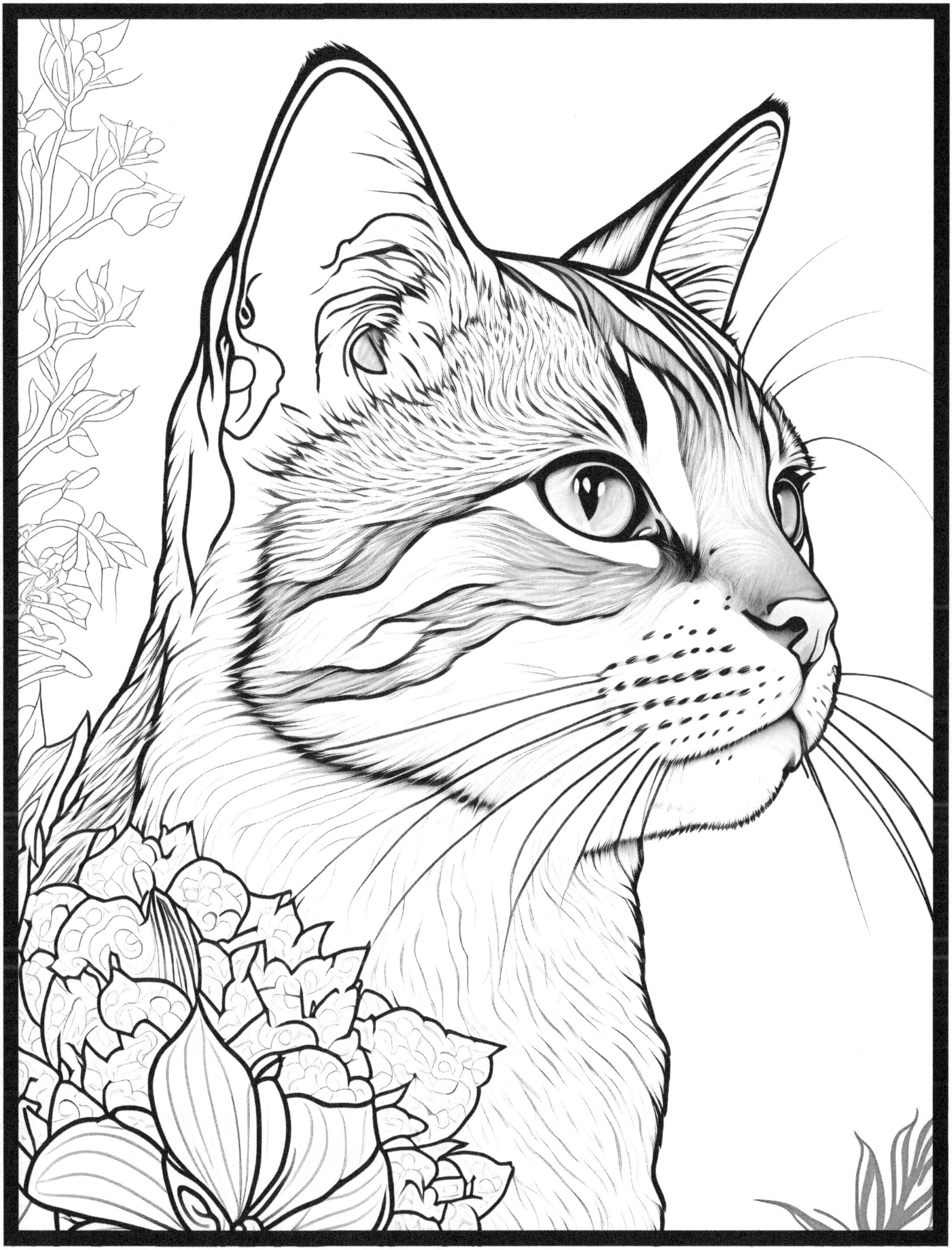

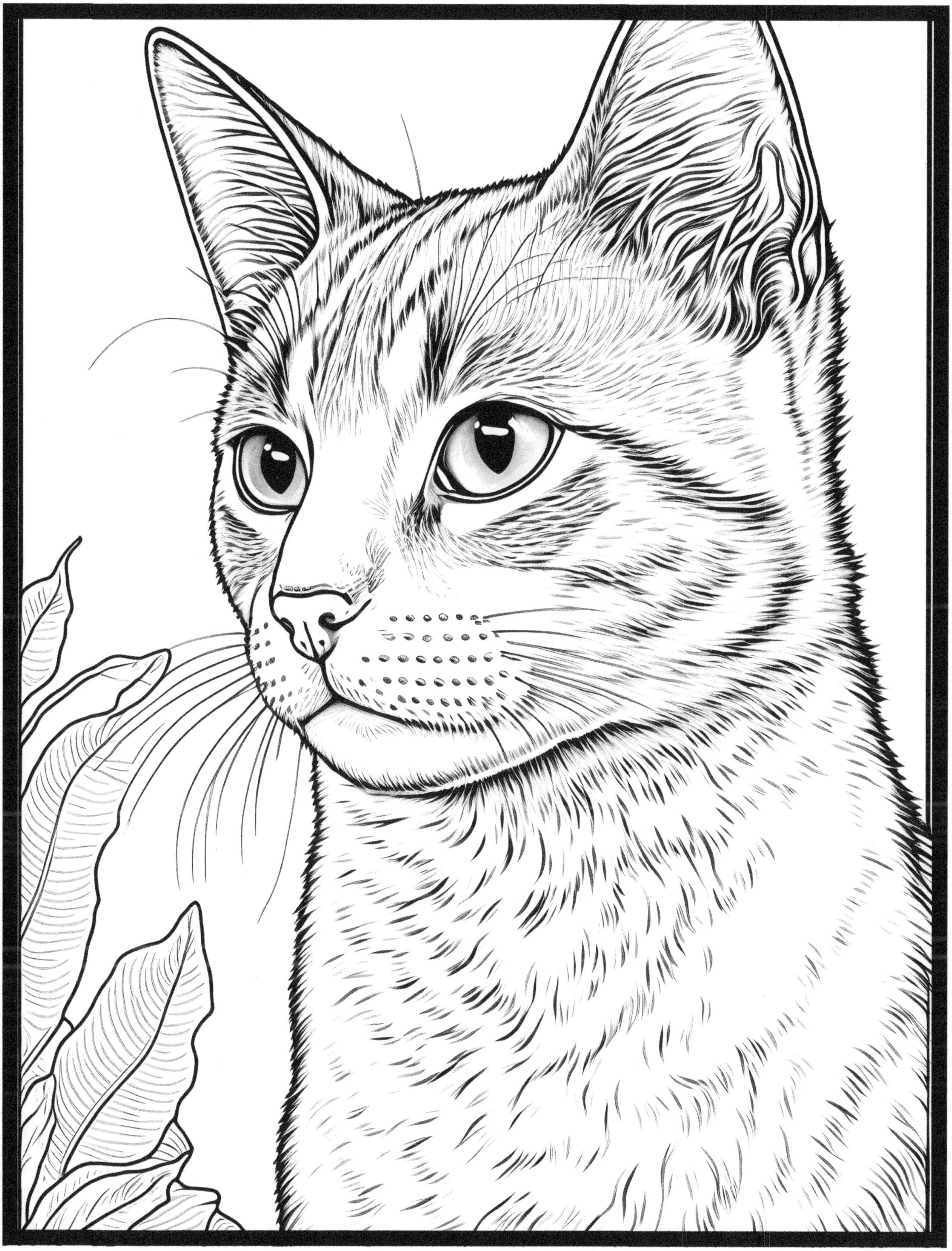

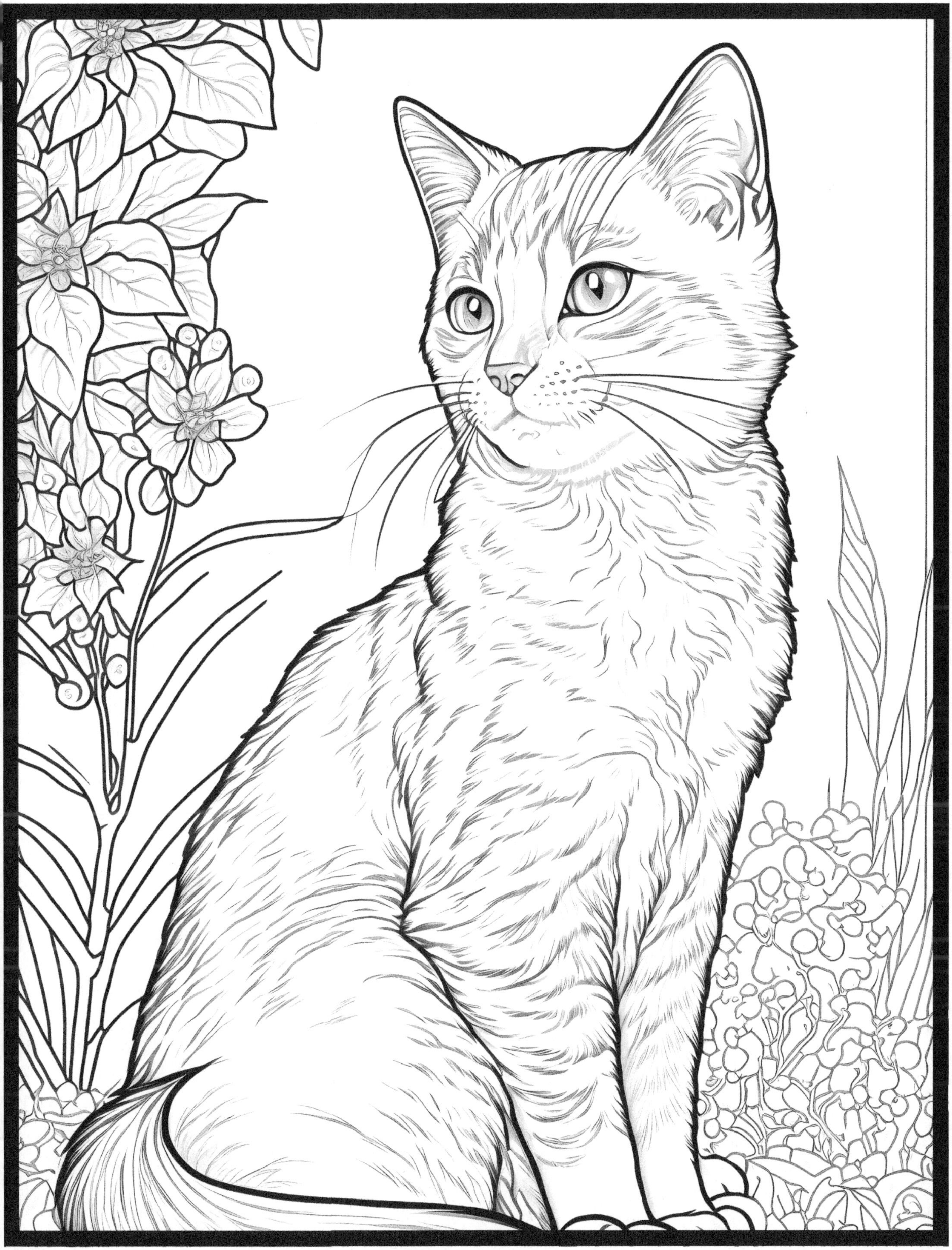

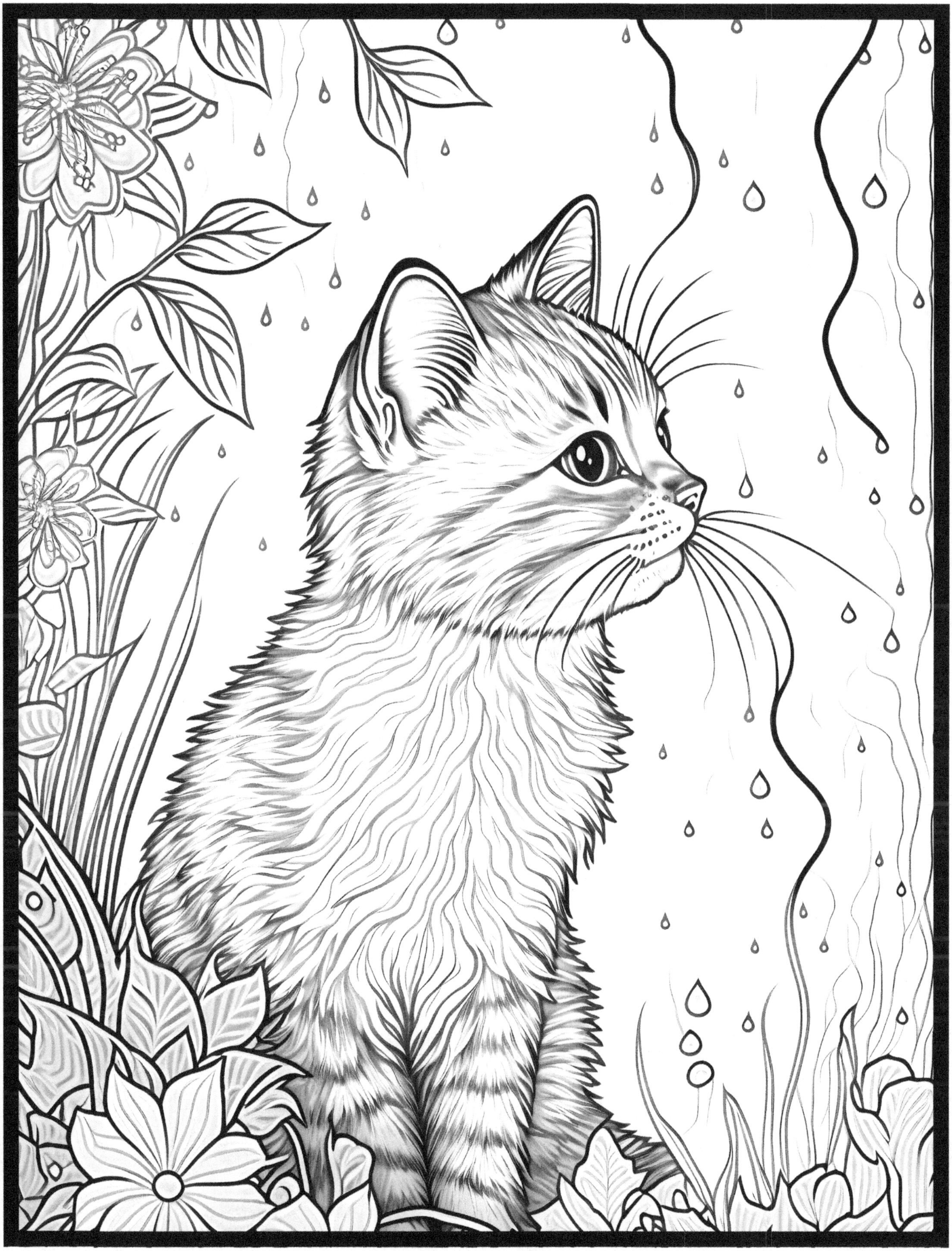

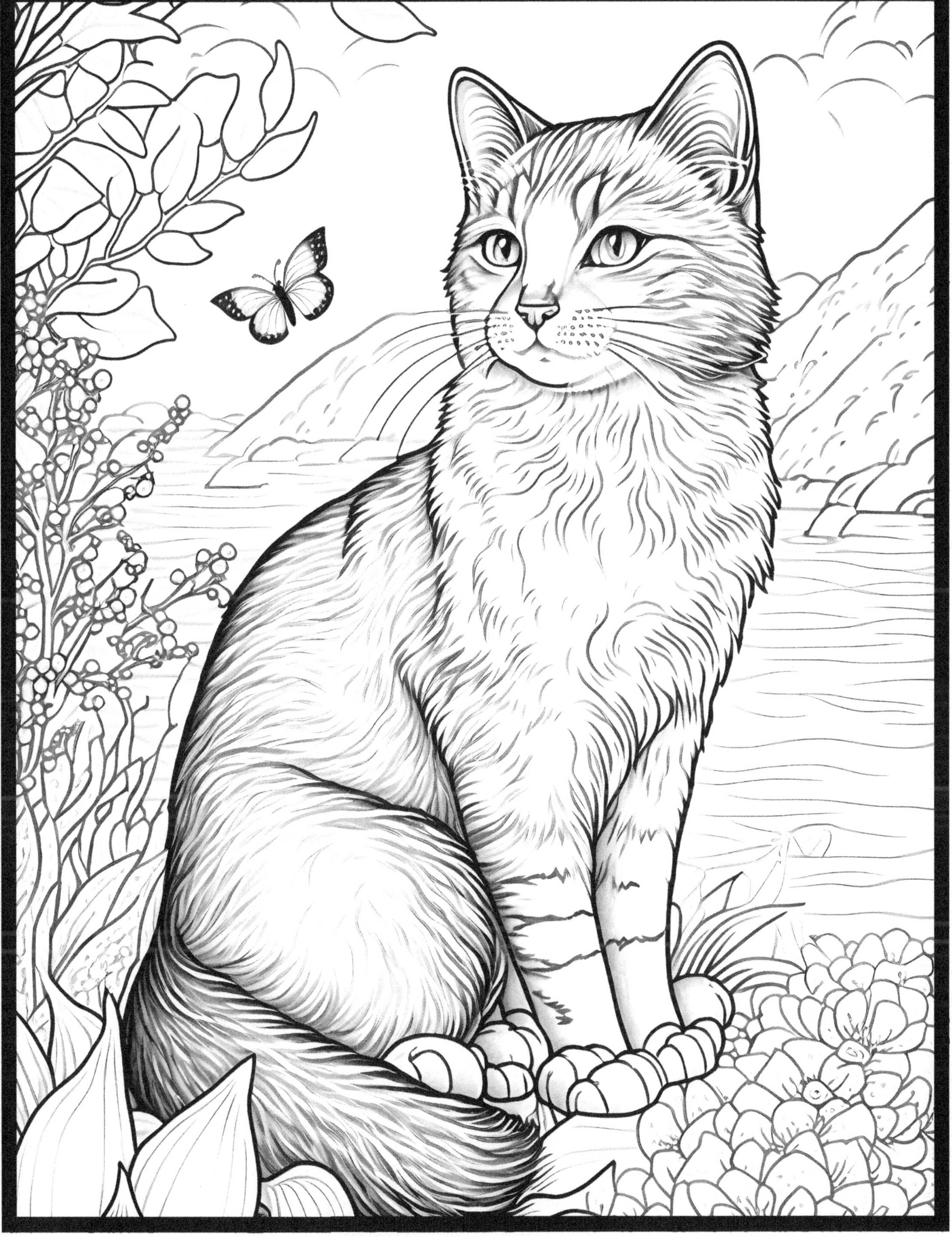

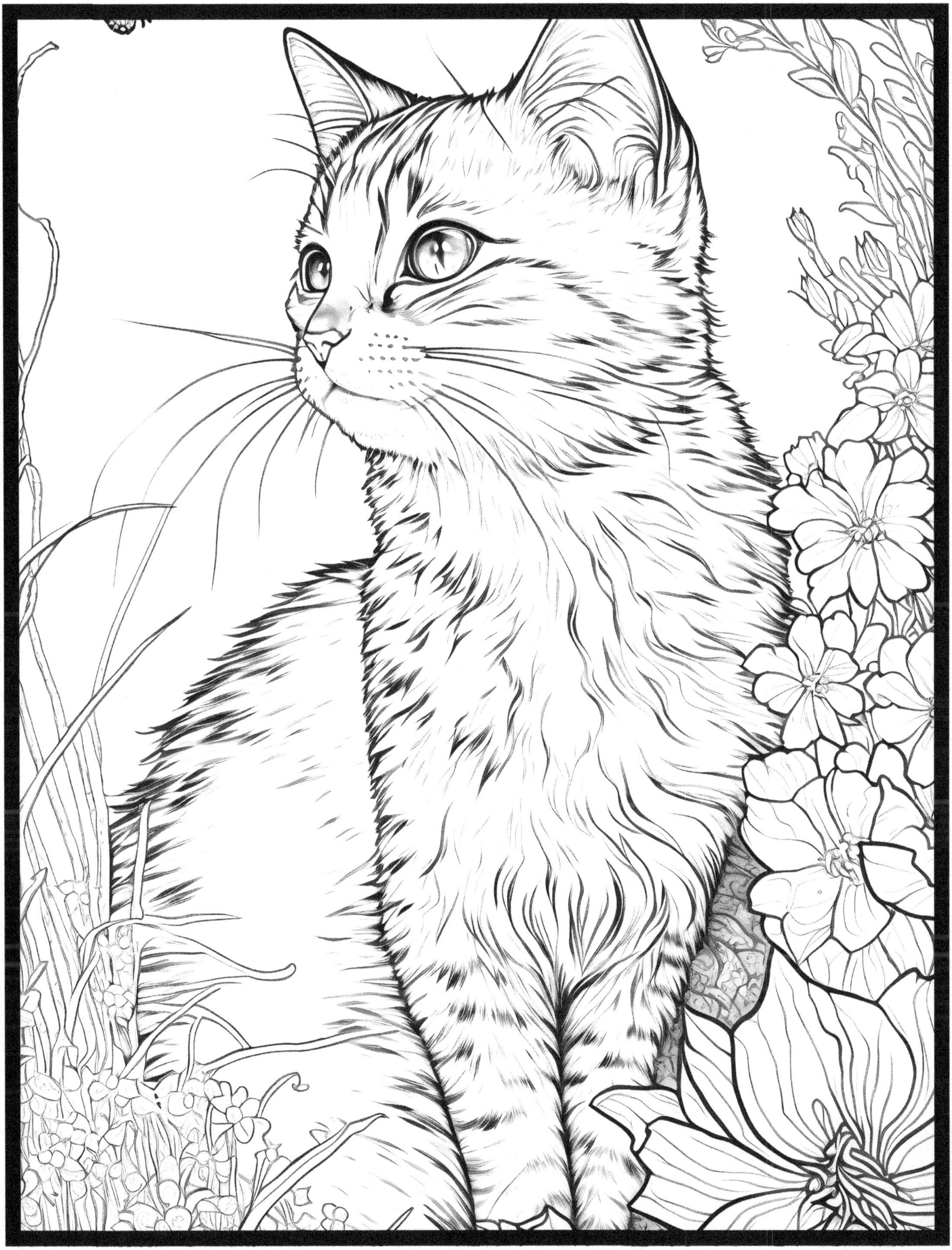

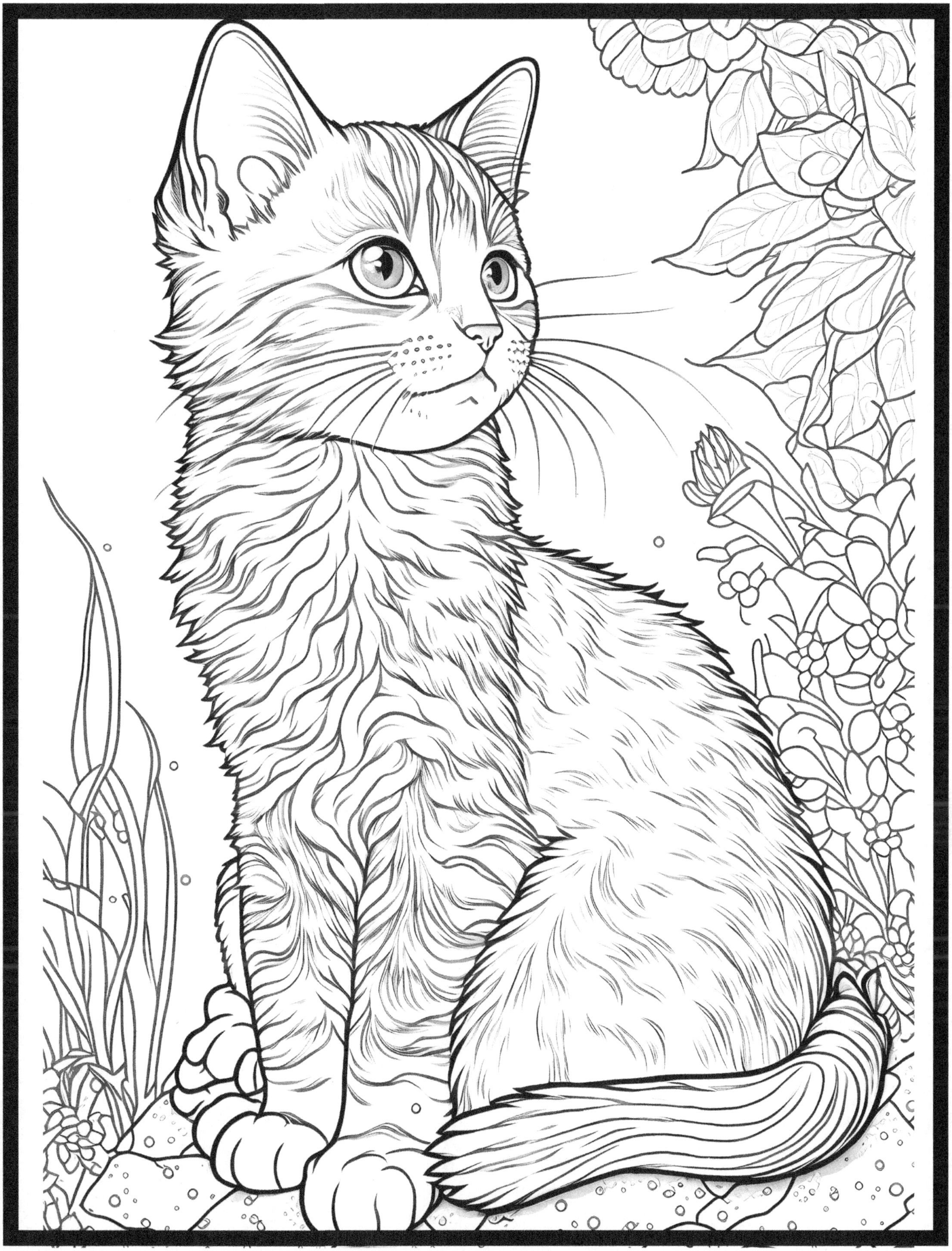

Made in the USA
Las Vegas, NV
05 December 2024

13378078R00024